Dear Jeanette

May the Lord

bless you richly!

Millie Mc M

# LOVE LETTERS
## *from*
# Heaven

MILDRED McMARTIN

LifeRich Publishing is a registered trademark of The Reader's Digest Association, Inc.

LifeRich Publishing books may be ordered through booksellers or by contacting:

LifeRich Publishing
1663 Liberty Drive
Bloomington, IN 47403
www.liferichpublishing.com
844-686-9607

ISBN: 978-1-4897-3450-1 (sc)
ISBN: 978-1-4897-3451-8 (e)

Library of Congress Control Number: 2021904512

Print information available on the last page.

LifeRich Publishing rev. date: 03/24/2021

Whatever I tell you in the dark,
speak in the light; and
what you hear in the ear,
preach on the housetops.

—Matthew 10:27 (NKJV)

# CONTENTS

# INTRODUCTION

This is a collection of prophecies received over a period of thirty-seven years.

Most of the words of encouragement were given to a local assembly of believers. A few are prophecies given to encourage an individual.

Each letter is an expression of the father's love and care for his individual children.

For those who have not known the father's love, reading the letters may convince them that the father is not distant or harsh, but in reality, he loves and tenderly cares for all the concerns of his children.

I suggest that the letters be read one at a time in order to appreciate each message more fully.

*Chapter 1*

# PROVISION

My dear child,

You are precious to me.

You are my chosen one.

I love you.

I love you just as you are.

You are a very special treasure to my heart.

Draw closer and closer to me.

Come close to me so you'll know my love for you.

Come close so I can lead you, teach you, and guide you as you are being changed by my love.

Follow close to me on the pathway I've chosen for you.

Do not strive and strain to be something you see in others.

You are who I want you to be.

I do not create duplicates.

You are unique.

You are special and one of a kind, not simply because I like variety but because I have a purpose, a plan, and a mission that can only be filled by you.

No one else can be my person for the purpose I am creating you.

Do not resist me, and do not look at another and desire to be them.

You are exactly as you are planned to be.

Do not resist my creative process.

Listen to me and obey me.

Walk the walk I call you to walk.

Walk close to me and listen to me.

Do not walk ahead and do not cower backward.

Walk with confidence, knowing that I walk with you.

I will hold your hand.

I will protect you, and I will provide you with all that you need for the walk I call you to walk.

I will provide you with all that you need. In addition, I will provide you with much joy because I'm well pleased and delighted with your obedience, and I want your joy to be full to overflowing.

Follow close to me on the pathway I've chosen for you.

Come walk with me, come talk with me, and know me more fully; you will not be disappointed, and you will increase my joy and my delight.

You shall walk in a way of victory through turmoil, on a path that my hand has prepared for you.

You shall take the glad tidings of my deliverance to people held captive in the darkness.

Remember my promise that the good work I have begun in you I will continue to bring to completion.

The gifts and calling of God are sure; they are not given and then taken back.

My giving is only limited or restricted by your willingness to obey me, by your willingness to walk humbly with me, and by your willingness to receive all that I have for you.

Come closer and receive my love, my power, and my discipline.

My dear child,

Your calling, gifts, and talents are not coincidences.

Realize that because you belong to me, you have a rich treasure inside you that people need.

I made you on purpose.

Never compromise, my child.

You are my masterpiece, my image bearer.

Know that you are the only you there has ever been or ever will be.

No one else looks, acts, or sounds like you.

I created you to be an original, not a copy. And you are not to be compared to others.

You are special to me, and I have a great future planned for you.

My beloved,

My love will meet all your needs.

Trust me.

My grace is sufficient, and my strength and power will be made manifest because of your weakness—not because of your wholeness.

Don't you know that it is out of your weakness and insufficiency that life and wholeness are brought forth and my grace and power are revealed?

Oh, how I love you! And my love will not let you be destroyed.

I have very special plans for you, and I am preparing you for a special purpose, with eternal goals in mind.

My beloved,

I am with you every moment of life and in every state that you find yourself.

I am with you when you're conscious of my presence and when, to you, I seem distant.

I am always with you.

I'm with you when you are busy with living and when you are at rest—when your mind is on me and when it is otherwise occupied.

I am with you always.

I'm with you to guide you, to give you wisdom, to comfort you, to give you strength, and to give you rest.

Never undertake a task or an endeavor without calling on me to enable you to do what is to be done.

I'll help you to pray, to praise, and to worship.

Your pleasing me is your life of worship. Walk in peace and in confidence, knowing that I am able to accomplish all that you commit to me.

Commit each day and all of its concerns to me and rejoice in my mercy, grace, and goodness to you.

My dear child,

I love you with an everlasting love.

I love you with an unchanging love.

I love you with a love that cannot be destroyed.

I love you with a love deeper than the ocean and wider than the sky.

I love you with a love that is stronger than death.

I love you with a love that is gentle and warm.

I love you with a love that is quiet and calm.

I love you with a love that forgives.

I love you with a love that seeks the best for you.

Do not fear my love.

Do not expect my love to be as people's love.

My love is unhindered.

As you learn to freely accept my love, you will also learn to let my love flow through you to others, unhindered by fear.

You will learn that I alone am the one to meet all your needs.

I alone am your security.

I alone am your life and your love.

Come to me, and come to know my love for you.

My love for you will heal your hurts.

My love for you will fill the emptiness in your heart.

My dear child,

My word is anointed with unlimited power.

My word will accomplish my purpose.

My purpose is that you come to me so that you might know me.

As you come to know me, you will become more like me.

As you know me, you will love me, obey me, worship me, and walk with me.

You will walk in confidence, love, joy, and peace.

My Holy Spirit applies my word to your heart and into your life.

All you supply is your willingness to hear, trust, and obey.

When you're willing to hear, trust, and obey, you will not be able to contain the blessings, so you will be a channel of my blessings and my provisions.

You will be a channel through which I will touch the lives of those you touch—to those you bring to me in prayer.

Fear not. I give you my peace.

Be strong. Yes, be strong and work, for I am with you.

I am the Lord of hosts.

Be strong and work the works I've prepared for you.

Be strong in me and in the power of my might.

My children,

My children, you have lifted to me empty hands.

It is because they have been held before me in their emptiness and in their weakness that I can fill them.

You lifted them to me.

You only weary yourself when your hands are kept down and you go about busying yourself, working things by the power of your own hands.

For the strength of my people will be to stand still and lift their hands to me.

Into your empty, weak hands I will pour out my strength and fullness. And my people will be a people to the praise of my glory, for they have learned that all things are of my doing and none of their own.

So rejoice in the confidence that you have reached unto me, and let your hands reach up not only in a token of request but in a token of receiving.

Let them be open to receive, for I, the Lord, will give as I have promised.

My dear child,

My child, I love you with an everlasting love.

I do not love as others do.

My love is pure love, with no mixture in it, with no ulterior motives.

I love because I am love.

My love for you is pure, deep, and boundless.

You can never fathom the depths of my love for you.

It is like the ocean: deep, wide, and mighty in power to heal.

You can hear about my love.

You can even see it being expressed.

But you must take off the death bindings of your past and step into my love, just as you would take off your clothes to step into the ocean.

And as a little child comes to the edge of the water, wet your feet and then sit in the shallows to delight in the refreshing waters.

So you must come to me and learn of my love.

Come to me often so you'll learn more and more of the delights of my love for you.

I love you, and I invite you to come into my love and learn of me.

Learn the depth and riches of my love for you so that you, in turn, might invite others to learn by experience the reality of my love.

My beloved child,

I know you and loved you before you were born.

I designed you to be my treasured child, to be my child of love.

I want you to know and experience my great love for you.

My love will fill those deep holes left in your heart where love was not delivered to you by those who should have loved you but were unable to receive or give love.

My love for you is so wide and deep that no matter how wide or deep those empty places are in your heart, they will be filled to overflowing.

My love for you will be more than you can contain and will overflow and splash onto those around you.

You will become a channel of my love and will bless many, for many are dying for the lack of love.

Receive my love.

My dear child,

My mercies are new every morning.

My mercy is everlasting.

My mercy is free.

You cannot pay for my mercy.

You cannot pay for my grace.

You cannot earn my love.

My love, my mercy, and my grace are deeper and wider than all the oceans, and they are freely offered to you.

Come to me and drink—drink of my love and my mercy, of my grace and my power.

There is more than you can possibly need.

There is more than you can use, so drink deeply from my living water and live.

Live the abundant life I've given you.

Drink deeply and be filled to overflowing with my love, and then go tell the thirsty, dying ones that I am the water of life.

Come, be filled with my love.

My beloved,

Hunger and thirst for me.

I am the bread of life, and I am the water of life.

Feast on me. Feast on my word. Drink and drink. You will always be satisfied, for I give you life.

I give in abundance all that you need to live this life today.

Rejoice. My supply never diminishes; it's always enough for all that you need.

Come to me moment by moment, keeping company with me throughout your day.

What you need, I offer it to you.

Learn to receive from me.

I love you so, and I want you to have my love and my provisions in abundance.

Rejoice and be glad!

My dear child,

No one can deliver from my hand.

Forget the past, for I am doing a new thing.

I know what I'm doing.

I govern human events for my purposes and according to my timetable.

I am working things out my way and in my time.

Believe me, child. I am in control even if I do not do things your way and in your time.

I am sovereign.

I control everything that touches your life.

Be patient, my child.

I am with you and will keep you safe, and I will strengthen you.

Do not look at the circumstances that would try to disquiet you.

Instead, fix your eyes on me and on my word to you.

I will not fail you.

Trust me, and wait with confidence and quietness.

You will see my hand sovereignly bring the victory, and you will see the victory as it unfolds, and you will rejoice in your God.

I am faithful and true, and I will be your confidence and your peace, your strength and your joy.

I will be your light in the darkness of the unknown.

Know this with certainty: I will not forsake you, and your child will not go begging.

I will hold you up, and I will provide all that you need.

My beloved,

Speak to them all that I have spoken to you.

Speak with confidence. Do not be timid.

Do not be ashamed or self-conscious.

Those who receive my word will be blessed.

Those who do not will suffer lack for having not received from me.

Speak—and leave the outcome in my hands.

The outcome is my concern, not yours.

My word is anointed with power to accomplish my purpose.

I carefully watch over my word and see to it that it brings about the purpose for which I send it forth.

I anoint you with my Holy Spirit and with power to accomplish my purpose and plan.

I carefully and jealously watch over my servants.

I protect them, and I supply their every need.

I'm so anxious to fill your every need that, at times, I pour out my treasure on you without your asking.

Other times, I desire for you to ask, not that I wish to withhold but that you may be encouraged to grow in love and gratitude and faith.

Do not hesitate to ask.

I'm just waiting for your request, and it fills me with joy to give you good gifts and gifts that are good for you.

My dear child,

I only want the very best for you, and as a result, I do withhold from you those things that are less than the very best.

Do not fuss or fret when you do not get your way. There is a good reason. I am your heavenly father, and I do not want you to bother with those things that are not good for you and could harm or hurt you.

I love you with a love that cannot be measured; it is wider, deeper, and higher than you can comprehend.

I have blessings on top of blessings for you—free gifts for the asking.

Come to me and ask. Ask, believing that I'm your heavenly father, who keeps his word, who is always available to you, with undivided attention, and who loves you with an everlasting love.

My love for you is not affected by how you look, by how you measure up, or by how you perform.

I love you because I love you.

Come close to me and learn more of how I love you.

My word reveals me. Feed on my word, and you will grow strong, and you will be healed, and you will be set free.

My beloved,

Walk by faith without seeing ahead. Step ahead with me as I direct one step at a time, one day at a time.

Don't be overconcerned with what was not done yesterday or what is to be done tomorrow.

Rejoice in my goodness, mercy, presence, guidance, grace, and all my provisions for today.

Walk by faith, counting on the fact that my word is true for you today.

My word changes not.

Is not your life greater than foof?

I will provide all that you need. Have I not done so all these years? *yes!*

You are complete in me.

You lack no good thing, and I will provide all that you need today and each day.

Trust me as you trusted me in years past.

Live before me with total openness and without shame.

Your days and years of shame are behind you; do not look back at them.

Live your life daily before me, having the righteousness that I have given you.

Be separated unto me from the world.

Glorify me!

My dear children,

My people, I love you.

How can I help you know how much I love you?

You are weary; I am your rest.

You are lonely; I am your companion, your friend, and your lover.

You are bound, shackled, and imprisoned; I am your liberator and deliverer.

Come to me and be free.

You are wounded and sick; I am your healer.

You despair; I am your comforter and your strengthener.

I am all you need.

I am the provider of all that you need.

Come to me and let me show you my great love for you.

Do not hesitate.

Do not say to yourself, "I'm not worthy."

I have made you worthy.

I have created you and am creating you.

I want your love, and you need my love.

So come to me. Come to me alone.

Come to me often. You will not be disappointed.

You will rejoice in my love, and your love for me will grow richer, deeper, and stronger.

As you come to me, you will be strengthened.

You will be equipped more and more to run the race and be victorious in the battle that rages all around you.

You will walk in victory, in confidence, and in safety.

Oh, yes, you may be wounded and scathed in the hand-to-hand scrimmages, but you will be triumphant in battle, for I have gained the victory, and you will claim that victory, and none can resist that victory won on Calvary.

Rejoice and be glad! Your king is all victorious!

Your king is coming soon!

Walk in victory and walk in love.

My beloved,

Come to me from your busyness.

Trim off the busyness of humankind's traditions.

Seek first my kingdom and my righteousness.

Seek to know me.

Seek to know and receive my love for you.

It is my love that is the core, the foundation, and the very root of all things in the abundant life.

The abundant life is not having all things your way.

The abundant life is having things my way.

My way of love brings life—abundant life and everlasting life.

My beloved,

I am your shield, comfort, and strength. I am yours forever.

Look past the mountains of obstacles.

Look steadfastly to me in my word.

There you will find peace, direction, and power to do the work I've called you to do.

I am Jehovah Jireh, and I will see to it that you have the provisions needed.

Be willing to yield to my way, and do not insist doing things your way.

My ways are not your ways.

Choose to trust me and obey me.

Your joy in me will be contagious.

Rejoice and be glad. Again, I say rejoice!

My beloved,

Do not fear. The battle is mine.

Enjoy my peace and rest easy.

Still your spirit and be quiet.

Be strong and work at yielding to my way.

I am with you. Remember that the victory and freedom from Satan's oppression is not by your might, power, and will; it is by my Holy Spirit, who is mighty to deliver and mighty to save.

Do not be weary in doing what you know is good and right.

Do this in the spirit of power I have given you.

My dear child,

Your position before me is important to you because it determines your service to me, as well as your communion with me.

Humble yourself before me, and I will lift you up and direct you in the way you are to go.

I will go with you and be your wisdom and your strength.

I will be all that you need me to be.

I will be your light and your joy.

I will be your all—your everything!

I will be your very life!

My dear child,

I love you with an everlasting love.

I have gifts of love I'm just waiting to pour out upon you—gifts of love to my church and gifts of love to you.

My gift to you is my love.

Love to fill your heart to overflowing.

Love your heart cannot contain.

Love that will bubble up from your inner being, from the living fountain I've put within you.

Receive from me with abandon; receive freely, and freely give of the love I give to you.

There is an inexhaustible supply.

I am love, and I cannot be contained or measured.

My love is powerful.

My love is healing.

My love is freedom.

My love is all that you need, for in my love is all that satisfies and all that fulfills.

You will receive more and more of my love, and you will share my love more and more with others.

But remember you must always come to me first, to receive from me, so that you can then go to others and give—then return for me to personally give to you.

Repeat this daily, and repeat this retreat as you did this week.

Come apart to me alone, to be loved personally by me for extended segments of time alone.

You will thus be refreshed, restored, and cleansed of the world's dust that clings to your feet.

You will thus be restored for the next part of your assignment in my vineyard.

Don't be anxious about what I'll have you do.

I'll give you all that you need to complete the task ahead.

Rest in me. Abide in me.

Trust me and promptly obey whatever I tell you to do, just as you are now, and I will teach you as you go.

P.S. I love you, my dear child. I see your heart, and you delight my heart!

My dear child,

I am faithful to my word.

Look to me and recall my word to you.

I will cleanse, I will heal, I will redeem, and I will set free.

Do not fear, for I am working the victory, and you shall see the victory.

Do not faint but stand firm, knowing that I will sustain and I will perform that which I have spoken.

The enemy knows he is defeated, but he delights in wearing down the saints. He is filled with glee to pounce on those who are shot down and wounded by fellow saints. These are the easy targets of his torments.

Despair not, for the very things meant for your defeat are used to enhance your inner strength, perseverance, and dependence on me.

Be still and know that I am God and that I am infusing you with strength that is not your own but mine.

Be still and do not faint.

Know that I am faithful and true, and know that I will not be mocked.

The haughtiness of humankind shall be made low, and your Lord alone will be exalted.

My beloved,

There is rest and rejoicing as you trust in me and rely on me and my faithfulness to my word.

Jesus has completed and fully accomplished his redemption of your spirit, soul, and body.

He has given you the Holy Spirit to be your in-resident counselor, teacher, comforter, and guide.

The Holy Spirit is my power working in you; he gives you power to love me and others, power to be a witness of what I've done in your life, and power to do all the good works I have planned for you to do.

When I ask you to do something for me, do not say, "I can't possibly do that." On your own, you can do nothing.

When you trust me and rely completely on me and the Holy Spirit in you, you can do all things through me.

Simply count on me to be all that you need, in order to do what I plan for you to do.

You are my instrument for my carrying out my plan.

Do not fear or be anxious.

Talk to me about everything, and I'll talk you through each and every task I give you.

Rejoice! You are not alone.

I am with you and will guide you and strengthen you as you cooperate with me in fulfilling my good plans for you.

My beloved,

Learn to depend on me.

Learn to involve me in all that you say and do.

Talk to me about everything—I mean everything: your waking, your sleeping, your daily activities of living, your working, your playing, your eating, your spending of time, and your spending of money.

Include me in all that you do.

I will not interfere; I want you to fully enjoy life, free of indecision, doubt, and fear.

I want you to enjoy my love, peace, joy, and all the good things I have for you.

My abundant life includes you living in me and allowing me to live through you.

I love you dearly and want you to receive and know my love for you more and more.

I want you to enjoy all that I have done for you and all that I do for you.

You are so precious to me!

*Chapter 2*

# PROTECTION

My beloved,

The Lord your God is in you and is mighty to deliver you from Satan's oppression, temptations, and traps.

My truth in you is powerful in setting you free from all that binds you and hinders you from running the race of life and walking the walk of faith.

My truth is the key to your freedom and your victorious living.

I will give you teachers who have been given nuggets of Revelation truth.

As you learn and apply these truths to your living, more and more truth will be given you.

The application of the truth and the practice of it will prepare you for more truth.

The hungry seeker of truth will never be disappointed as he or she lives my word in obedience.

Life becomes more and more satisfying and exciting as you see me accomplish my word in you and through you day by day.

My beloved,

My child, you are in a race and a battle, and I will see to it that you win both.

Just as in a race, the runner is supplied with nourishing liquids as he runs, and in a battle, the fighting troops are supplied with nourishment and ammunition supplies, I am supplying you with nourishment and supplies you need to run the race and win the battle.

There are times in a race when the runner comes to level ground, where he is able to increase his strength and energy, and in a prolonged battle, there are times of less intensity, when the soldiers are able to get their bearings, tighten their belts, and ready themselves for the next onslaught.

I provide such times for my children, who are in the race of life and on the battlefield against the enemy.

Remember at the end of the race and the battle, you are victorious. You win!

In the meantime, know that you have a great crowd of witnesses watching and cheering you on, and all the while, you have your Savior and the Holy Spirit interceding on your behalf.

My dear child,

Do not fear the wrath of humankind.

I am a jealous God.

I am a consuming fire.

I will utterly destroy that which raises itself above me.

You will have no other gods before me.

There is no God beside me.

Some trust in wealth and bribes.

They are emptiness and cannot stand.

They are nothing.

Your position before me is what is of value.

You are of great value to me, for I see your heart, whether it be fully yielded to follow as I lead or stubborn and self-willed.

My dear child,

We are at war twenty-four seven.

Be sure to wear the armor—that is, the truth of my word applied to your daily living.

As Jesus used the word to defeat the enemy, so must you declare my word each time the destroyer attempts to feed you his lies.

You must counter his every negative bait by declaring my word of truth.

Feed on my word daily so it becomes ready on your mind and in your mouth.

My dear child,

Do not despair, and strive not.

I protect you, and I gently lead you.

Let go of yesterday and your failings of yesterday.

Today, I give you a new gift. It's a brand-new day, and again today, my mercies are new for you.

My grace uses your yesterday for good—your good and the good of others.

Fret not, because I have taken care of yesterday, and it is now history; you must not touch it again.

Now is the day to live, love, rejoice, and be my beloved.

You are my beloved. Nothing can change that—nothing. I am delighted in you.

I'm delighted by the fact that you seek me, seek to know me, and want to be led by me.

I rejoice in your thanks and your praises, and I especially like it when you say, "The Lord says …" followed by what I've said.

You are under my wings, you are in the palm of my hand, and you are securely in my heart.

I love you dearly.

Know my peace.

My dear child,

Yield to me.

Yield to me as I work out in you that which I purpose for you.

You are my precious child.

You have all my love and all my attention.

I give to you all that is mine.

I yearn for you to give all of yourself to me.

You are mine, and I love you with an everlasting love.

Come to me and give yourself to me completely.

I will not disappoint you.

I want you to live in the fullness of my love, joy, and peace.

My dear child,

Fix your eyes on me.

You have heard correctly.

Do not look about.

Keep your eyes on me.

My plans for you are for good, not evil.

Trust me with your whole heart.

You shall not be disappointed.

Deeds not of me will be exposed to the light.

I will open their eyes, and they will repent and turn from their wicked ways.

You serve the mighty God of the universe.

The devil cannot overtake you.

The devil cannot destroy you, for you belong to me.

Their deeds will prosper for a while.

But I will expose them, for I am God, and I cannot be mocked.

So hold onto your faith.

I guarantee they will be exposed. They shall be ashamed, and they shall repent, and they shall understand.

I will not be mocked.

You come into the Sabbath rest and watch me move soveignly.

I have set you free.

I have set you free so that you might help me set others free from prisons that Satan has ensnared them in—those things that shackle them and hinder their walk with me.

I have revealed to you, through others, my truth in my word that sets the captive free.

I will use you to spread the good news, that knowing my truth indeed sets you free of many things that have had control over you.

Review your own deliverance.

Be at peace as you study and know more and more about your own deliverance.

It will be a source of much joy and rejoicing.

My dear child,

You are not where you were last week.

You have been through much—much devastation.

When this comes again, you will not react in the same way, for you are growing.

You will not be devastated in your spirit.

"No weapon formed against you will prosper."

My word will guard your heart, and you will not respond the way you responded in the past.

My word is guarding your heart.

This is a new step of growth, a new step of faith.

You will not weep, but you will have joy—unspeakable joy in the midst of trial.

For my word is taking root in your heart.

You will not be flip-flopping up and down, for you will have the word when things come against you.

Much devastation has crushed you in the past, but from now on, your response will be much different.

My dear child,

You are my beloved child.

Listen to my word.

I will direct you, love you, comfort you, correct you, and protect you. But you must come to me.

Listen to what I say to you personally before you go out to speak to and minister to others.

Unless you hear my word, my voice to your own heart, how are you to have any living water for those who thirst?

Come to me alone and hear my word to your heart.

Come to me, and I'll speak to you of my love for you, and you'll learn that my grace is sufficient for all that you need.

Come, my child. Listen to me, and I will teach you the fear of the Lord.

My beloved,

As you diligently seek to know me, I will reveal myself to you.

You will learn to know more and more of my love.

But you will also learn more and more of my holiness and power, of my good plans for you, and of my ways of bringing about my will for you.

I know you're excited and full of zeal for me and my plans, but be patient, for my timing and my preparations are exactly what is needed to bring forth my good plans for you and for those to whom you are called to minister.

Be at peace, knowing I have all things in my control and I will lead you each step of the way—my way.

Rejoice, for I am pleased at your willingness to follow me and walk humbly with me.

My dear child,

I am the Lord your God, the holy one.

I am your Savior.

I am the faithful one.

I am the Lord, and besides, me there is no savior.

You are not your own.

You are the temple of the living God.

I live in you.

I'm closer than a brother or wife or husband.

Do not look to others.

Look to me in your need.

I am your comforter.

I'm your encourager.

I am the all-sufficient one.

Call on me at all times, and I will answer you.

Learn to rely on me and on my word.

I will not disappoint you.

I love you.

You are mine, and I love you.

My dearest one,

Give me your heart, your broken heart.

Place it in my hands.

I will heal it.

I will strengthen it.

I will soften the scars.

Your heart will become whole and healthy; it will be restored, and your heart will be a heart of love.

You will be able to love and be loved, and you will rejoice in my love.

Do not look back.

Do not probe the scars that cover your heart.

I will even heal the scars so that they will not hurt when touched.

I am the healer of broken hearts.

Give me your heart, your heart of hearts.

Yes, I can even heal those deep, secret wounds, even those wounds that you are not fully aware of—those wounds that cause you to be crippled in relationships.

Hand me your heart, and I will restore it. I will give it to you again, full of love, and it will be a channel of my love to those who desperately need love, to those who are about to die for the lack of love—for the lack of my love.

I love you with a love you cannot comprehend.

You can learn to receive more and more of my love.

You can learn to be a channel of my love.

Rejoice in my love as I rejoice in your love for me.

Come to me often, to receive special touches of my love for you personally.

I love you. Be filled to overflowing with my love.

Some wounds you do not remember, but those wounds hinder your relationships now.

Even the buried wounds I will heal, and you will rejoice in new relationships and a new freedom of loving and being loved.

Do not fear. I am love!

My dear child,

The Lord is in his temple.

Let all the people be silent.

Enter my gates with thanksgiving.

Enter into my courts with praise.

Come before me and hear.

Come to listen, and you will hear if you quiet your racing spirit and still your voices.

Come to me and be still.

Oh, my people, keep silent and be still.

Hear my voice; it is not the shout but the whisper you hear in your heart.

Be still and hear my still, small voice, for I have much to tell you.

But you cannot hear, for you are too busy, too noisy, too agitated.

Be still, and you will know that I am God.

My dear child,

Yield to me.

Yield to me as I work out in you that which I purposed for you.

My dear child,

You delight in the beauty of my creation.

Look to me. Delight in me.

Focus on the beauty of my holiness, my awesome wisdom and power, and my unbounded love and grace to you.

Do not doubt my love for you.

Do not doubt my power to bring good out of the injustice and evil about you.

Put blinders on, focus your eyes on me, and worship your God.

Will you not tremble at my presence?

Look to me, not that which is evil.

Do you not know that I will even use that which is evil to bring about my purposes?

Fret not about those who prosper in their evil way.

I am a holy and just God, and I will make right that which is crooked.

Look only to me, and I will teach you to walk in my way, and we shall be one.

My dear child,

Your desire to know me and to yield your all to me is that which will bring new revelation of myself to you.

My mercies are new every morning, and so are your opportunities to learn of me.

Know that I love you, and I yearn to be known by you.

As you know me more, so your love for me and for others will grow.

As you personally know my love, your life will be filled with that love, and you will not be able to contain it—so my love will overflow and touch those you touch in your everyday living.

There is no effort involved, for it is an overflow of my love in you.

My dear child,

Be still, my child. Rest in my arms.

You are safe and secure, for I watch over you.

I have good plans for you.

I love you with an everlasting love.

My power will be made known through your weakness and limitations.

My wisdom and power have no limits.

Rest in me. Rely fully on my love and my power to save and heal, to deliver from the plans of the enemy.

Rejoice and be glad.

*Chapter 3*

# DIRECTION

My dear child,

Time is brief, my child, but it has the power of determining how you spend eternity.

Your choices and your priorities here and now will influence the quality of your eternal life.

The Holy Spirit and my word will guide you as you seek to know me and my way for you.

Listen for my voice.

I will guide you safely home.

My dear child,

Time is short, so use each day to show the world around you some likeness of your Savior.

How will people in your life know the love of God unless you show them?

It cost Christ his very life to show you the father's love.

Are you willing to pay the cost of showing people the love of God?

The cost may be for you to put another's needs before your own.

It may cost you humility to ask for forgiveness when you have wrong someone.

It may cost you the approval of humankind in order to have the approval of God.

My dear child,

Do not pick up and carry another's burden.

Instead, hold each one and their need up to me in prayer.

I've called you to rest in me.

Rest in my love, in my power, and in my protection.

I will direct your steps as you continue to seek my face.

Continue to obey me, that your joy may be full and overflowing.

My beloved,

Be still. Be confident in me. Be steadfast and unmovable.

I've made you my own, and I am making you a new instrument for my purposes—to encourage others in their walk with me, their relationship with me, and their intimacy with me.

Do not draw back from those very different from yourself.

Focus on them and their needs and on your yielding to my promptings concerning them.

Remember, the motive for your relationship with anyone and everyone you meet is love—my love for them.

My purpose for each one is to love them and draw them to myself, with my love and my power working in you and in them.

My love and my truth work together. They cannot work independently, though it is my love that draws them to the truth.

Love prepares the heart to receive the truth.

My beloved,

Be silent, my child.

When you speak, let it be your heart that calls my name.

Many have my name upon their lips, but their hearts are hollow shells.

Love is not in a mouth that is full but in an overflowing heart.

It is with the heart that man believes unto righteousness, and with his mouth he confesses salvation.

No mouth shall testify of salvation and speak the truth until first the heart has believed unto righteousness. I listen for the words of your heart.

I understand the language of love.

He who speaks only with his mouth speaks a language that in heaven is unknown.

Even so, my child, when you listen for my voice, listen with your heart.

The ears listen with curiosity; the heart listens with obedience.

Be that one who listens with the heart.

Be that one who is tuned to my father's will and understands the language of heaven.

My dear child,

Your Savior has given you power of attorney—authority to use his name against all the works of Satan.

Be alert and ready to cast down every assault by the enemy forces.

Defeat the lies with the word of truth.

My dear child,

Like a boat without sails is cast about without direction and without power, my people without praise are subject to wayward winds, conflicts, distress, and damage.

In order to praise, there must be a focus on the one praised.

You cannot truly praise someone you do not know.

Look to me, consider me, and acknowledge my love for you.

As you know me, you will praise me.

Your heart must be turned to me in order to praise and worship me, or your praise is an empty performance of religion.

Religious performance, no matter how zealous or strenuous, is an empty work of the flesh and cannot be praise.

Humble, contrite hearts are hearts filled with gratitude, praise, and worship.

Quietly consider me and my love for you, and the thanksgiving, praise, and worship will be the result of your quiet contemplation.

You will not be able to restrain or contain your praise. It will freely flow from a grateful heart—sometimes as a breath of thanks and sometimes in joyful glee, in a loud exclamation, a song, a melody without words, and a joyous anthem that thrills your whole being.

Come to me and learn of me, to know my love for you.

My beloved,

Be not disturbed by evildoers.

They are in my hand, even as are the righteous.

I have certain things to accomplish that could not be brought to pass without this avenue of operation.

Do not be alarmed.

All is under my control.

Stand upon my word.

Let your only support be your faith in me.

I myself will hold you up.

I myself will keep you from swaying.

Do not be distressed by what goes on in others' lives.

I will deal with them and indeed can do so effectively only as they turn to me alone.

Your help is not needed and may be a detriment.

Their path is different from yours, and you cannot join them on their path.

My will and my best for you is your path.

Live in me, walk in me, and walk with me.

Counsel with me.

Look to me alone for your direction and encouragement.

I will minister to you as you wait upon me, as you seek my face, and as you search my word.

I know precisely what you need.

I will give you exactly what you need for health of soul and strength of spirit.

Go your way in peace and rejoice! The Lord your God is with you and will be your help.

My dear child,

You will worship Jesus forever.

You now worship him with a lifestyle that pleases him.

All that you do to please him is your worship.

So learn to do all things as an act of worship.

Do your daily chores as an act of worship, because they are.

Every thought and action brings glory or shame to his name.

Because you are his, you and all you do brings pleasure or the lack of it to him.

Do all to his glory and for his pleasure.

Your waking and sleeping, your speech, your use of time and your energies—all of these can be your conscious worship of him.

Even as a little child brings delight to her parents when she demonstrates her willingness to please, so your Redeemer and I rejoice when you demonstrate your willingness, your effort, and your desire to be and do what pleases us.

You are part of a growing family, and you are much loved.

My dear child,

Continue taking every opportunity you see to love and encourage others.

Continue being sensitive to others' needs.

Continue doing as I instruct you to do.

Your acts of kindness and love are not in vain.

I have told you to build others up, and each little act of love does just that.

No act motivated by love is ever in vain.

A look, a wave, a word, a hug, a hand on the arm or shoulder, each of these conveys my love to others.

This is your purpose—to love others on my behalf.

This includes words spoken at the best time.

I'll give you the right words, and I'll give you the best timing.

Your gentleness and my power will accomplish my purposes.

Continue being my blossom, putting forth the fragrance of my loving-kindness to others and bearing my fruit that strengthens and refreshes others.

My beloved,

I am the light of the world.

I call you to come to me.

Come to me. Let my light shine into your heart.

Come to me and know rest.

Come to me and know cleansing and refreshment.

Come to me. Be cleansed and made whole.

Enter into my life and allow me to live through you.

My dear child,

My good news is to be spread by each one who has been made alive in Christ.

The good news is your very own testimony of the good things I've done in you and in your life.

The good news is the written word spoken.

My words will always accomplish my purpose.

You are not responsible for the outcome of your sharing.

You are responsible for sharing what I have given you.

I will lead you and direct you in your sharing.

Do not be concerned about how and when.

I will direct you by the Holy Spirit.

Be courageous and fear not.

To be a spreader of my good news, you do not have to be perfect.

Your heart must be right with me, and I'll enable you to be the instrument in my hand to accomplish my purposes.

I am the one who does the work, but I do depend on my servants to be responsive to my spirit.

Give the good news of my power and of my love to those who have not known my love and feel powerless.

Tell them of my love and of my power to change lives.

My beloved,

The marriage of the Lamb draws near.

In great anticipation, the bride is being prepared for that great day.

All things must be clean and in their proper place.

All things must be made ready.

The bride is being prepared for the groom.

The groom waits in great anticipation.

She is being clothed in righteousness—new and spotless garments inside and out.

As the day approaches, the bride waits and watches for news of any sign that tells her time is near. It will not be long.

The trumpet is ready.

The groom's house is near completion.

Soon the word will be given, "Now go and bring the bride so we can celebrate the marriage of the Lamb."

My dear child,

My sheep hear my voice.

I speak softly and clearly.

Tune your heart to hear my voice.

Listen quietly.

Be still and know my voice.

I speak to you all day long, to tell you of my love and to give you direction.

You'll hear me if you listen with the intent of obeying me.

My beloved,

Yes, I do work all things together for your good.

I've called you for my purposes.

I will call you to be my person, to represent me in your world.

This means you are to live as I would live in your world.

This means you are to live with my love and my attitude toward all you have contact with.

Love, mercy, and grace are to be your characteristics.

You are to keep your word as I keep my word.

Do not speak quickly or carelessly.

Never speak in haste or in hostility toward others.

Let your speech be always seasoned with grace, no matter what the other's attitude is toward you.

Let gratitude and joy and peace be dominant in your thoughts and in your words.

Listen attentively so you will learn from others what they value and what they need most.

You cannot help everyone outwardly, but you can hold them and their need before me and ask for my intervention.

Leave the details up to me. Leave the how and the when up to me.

I will let you know if and when I want you to say or do anything to meet another's need.

Watch, pray, and wait on me.

My dear child,

My loving-kindness is everlasting.

My mercies are new for you every morning.

I love you with an everlasting love.

Why is it so hard for you to trust me?

Have I not always kept my word?

Have I not always been faithful in keeping my promises?

My plan for you is a good plan.

My ways are higher than your ways.

I love you, and I will not hurt you.

Oh yes, it may hurt for a while to realize that what you thought was my plan for you was really not my plan.

My love will meet all of your needs.

Trust me. My grace is sufficient, and my strength and power will be made manifest because of your weakness—not because of your wholeness.

Don't you know that it is out of your weakness and insufficiency that life and wholeness are brought forth and my grace and power are revealed?

Oh! How I love you!

My love will not let you be destroyed.

I have very special plans for you, and I am preparing you for a special purpose with eternal goals in mind.

Yield to me as I work out in you that which I have purposed for you.

You are my special child.

You are so precious!

You think I have so many children that you don't really count that much.

But you are as if you were my only child.

You have all my love and all my attention, and I give to you all that is mine.

I yearn for you to give all of yourself to me; hold nothing back from me.

You are mine, and I love you with an everlasting love.

Come to me and give yourself to me completely.

I will not disappoint you.

I want you to live in the fullness of my love, my joy, and my peace.

My dear child,

Do you collect and store little irritations and fretful things?

Deal with each one as it occurs; get it right with me and be rid of it.

It's these little foxes that gnaw away at your peace and integrity and your good witness to those around you.

Sin is a sin; confess it, turn from it, and ask for help in recognizing it and resisting it.

The war is heating up, and the enemy uses every opportunity to infiltrate and do his dastardly deeds to bring you down.

Seek discernment of Satan's tactics and defeat him before he gains access.

Though he has been defeated, he still steals, kills, and destroys.

He goes on in his denial of his defeat at the cross and empty tomb.

Be alert. Be vigilant. Watch and pray.

My beloved,

You withstand the enemy of your soul with the armor and weapon I have given you.

Stand victorious over all the lying and scheming the devil tries to trip you up with.

Be ready to go against his obvious and blatant attacks as well as against his subtle, sneaky invasions on your life.

You are victorious and remain victorious as long as you wear the armor, hold the shield of faith in place, and are ready with the word—your offensive weapon.

Know who you are and practice righteousness and truth.

Speak with the authority I have given you in the name of Jesus.

Rely on my faithfulness and my power.

Rely on me to be all and everything you need to be more than a conqueror.

You do not just get by; you win decisively.

You do not just break even; you excel.

You are a mighty warrior.

You are a winner.

You are mine.

Never revert to the old identity of victim.

You were victimized, but that is history never to be repeated in you.

You can remember but only for the purpose of encouraging and empathizing with victims who need encouragement and hope—the same hope that I've given you.

Remember all the ways I have brought you from darkness to light; from hopelessness to hope and expectation of only good things; from mourning to joy; from dark, ugly depression to beauty and wholeness; from weakness and wanting to strength and vibrant health and love of living.

Be ready to gently share my goodness to you with the broken, weak, and discouraged ones.

My beloved,

As the darkness deepens, your uprightness and integrity will be more and more noticed by those encouraged by it and those who oppose you.

Do not be distracted.

Keep focused on me and on the task I've given you.

You have a purpose that only you can fulfill.

Focus your attention, strength, and time on being a witness of my goodness to you, being my representative, my ambassador, my priest to your personal world—your family, friends, and neighbors. This is your mission field.

Continue the task I've given you.

Continue to love and encourage those I put on your path.

Above all else, continue to seek me and my ways by studying my word and yielding to the Holy Spirit as he guides you and instructs you on how and when to move forward in the mission I have given you.

Do not be anxious about any aspect of your mission.

I will lead you, and I will be your strength to walk the walk I have planned for you.

Do not falter or be overwhelmed, for I will work in you and through you as you seek me and as you continue to please me by depending on me to meet all your needs.

I love you, and your hunger to know me blesses my heart.

My dear child,

I will use you, but you will not be popular.

You love them as I direct you and leave their response to me.

Do not be concerned about how they respond to the love you show them.

Love the hurting ones.

Love the lonely ones.

Love them to life.

Encourage each individual you have contact with.

My love cannot be contained, just as my joy cannot be contained.

I've given you joy, and there is much, much more.

Come, receive my love and then let it flow through you to those I give to you.

My dear children,

You are my trees planted by the water.

My trees—oaks of righteousness.

Stand firm in what I have told you.

My ways are higher than your ways.

Stand firm and see the salvation of your Lord.

Do not receive what humankind tells you.

Receive what I tell you in my word.

I am not a man that I should lie.

My dear child,

The Lord your God in the midst of you is mighty.

Do not doubt my words to you.

I am true to my word, and I am all-powerful, and I will fulfill my word to you.

The way is long. It is my way, so do not fear.

You are in my hand.

I will do that which pleases me.

Trust me as I work out all the details. Nothing I do is superfluous.

Continue to receive from my hand, for all things are from me or are permitted by me.

They all have a purpose—a good purpose—so do not despair.

Your expectation is for me, and so it should be.

I work all things together for good.

Trust me and do not give up, for you will see my victory and my loving-kindness to you.

You feel the pain and not understand, but you will, and the intensity of your pain will be a means of ministering hope to others.

Your pain and your waiting are not in vain. Though now you cannot understand, one day you will.

Be still and know that I'm working in you that which will be used by me for my purposes—purposes you cannot begin to imagine.

Trust me and do not draw back from me as I continue my preparation of my servant.

My beloved,

Do not despair.

Trust me simply because you know that I'm faithful and I do not lie.

You will soon see my victory over sin and death, and you will see the captives free.

You, too, will enter freedom you have not yet known.

Do not fear the silence, for I am with you; you are not alone.

Cling to my word, for it does not change.

I will open my word to you more and more as you seek to know me.

You know in part, but your knowledge of me will grow as you yearn more and more to be one with me.

Look for my love in all you read in the word.

My beloved,

Whatever troubles you, whatever causes you to be ill at ease, bring it to Jesus. He is your burden bearer.

Bring it to him in prayer. Tell him what it is and give it to him.

The burden will still be yours, but he will carry the weight of it for you.

The Holy Spirit will give you wise counsel, strength, and guidance as to how you are to walk through the problem and come out victoriously.

Do not hold on to what seems to be small or insignificant.

You can accumulate those little things that trouble you until they weigh you down and trip you up on your journey.

Learn to turn them over to Jesus so that you can walk freely and unencumbered.

My beloved,

I am God.

I'm also your husband.

I will not forget or forsake you, for you are a child of my love.

I loved you before you were born.

I loved you at your birth and told you to live.

I betrothed you to me, and I'm fashioning you as a bride prepared for her bridegroom.

Do not be waylaid with incidentals.

Draw from me all that you need and all that you desire.

I will fulfill your deepest desires. Do not fear, for I walk with you to guide and to strengthen and to protect.

Remember, I know you, and I love you dearly.

My beloved,

In Christ, you can do all things I call you to do—to walk uprightly.

In Christ, you are victorious overcomers of the world, the flesh, and the devil.

You can and do overcome each of these, not by your own effort and will but by my Spirit—by relying on my might and my power.

The same power that raised Christ from the grave raises you from your dead works—your futile efforts.

Your old self died with Christ.

You must allow your old self to stay dead daily by living your new life in Christ.

Overcome the dead with life.

Overcome evil with good by starving the demands of the old nature and feeding the new person with new food.

Christ is the bread come down from heaven.

Daily feed on the living word to nourish and strengthen your new person— the spiritual person—the eternal part of you.

My word taken and spoken in faith and in believing is your means of overcoming and resisting the world's attitudes, sinful habits of your flesh, and the lies of Satan.

Practice moment by moment using my word, speaking it out loud each moment you're tempted to agree with or go along with the idea put in your head by the liar and his workers of destruction.

Be alert on purpose. Be deliberate in not going on mindless autopilot— doing what you've done so many times that it's automatic without conscious thought.

My beloved,

I will help you appropriate your redemption, all that was accomplished through the faith, obedience, suffering, bleeding, and death of Jesus and his resurrection.

You have begun to realize what was accomplished on your behalf, and you think it's almost too good to be true, but you know that my love for you is without measure.

You can believe and you do believe my word.

I will lead you into the richness of your redemption.

Always remember that our relationship is top priority, and all else flows from it.

Do not be anxious or overwhelmed with the immensity of my provisions for you.

Simply walk in obedience and reliance on me, and you will walk in victorious peace.

Let peace rule your heart.

When peace seems to withdraw, draw close to me, and peace will again envelop you.

Relax. You are in my hand, and I will never let you go.

My dear child,

My sheep hear my voice.

I speak softly and clearly.

Tune your heart to hear my voice.

Be still and know my voice.

I speak to you all day long, to tell you of my love and to give you direction.

You will hear me if you listen with the intent to obey me.

My beloved,

I will grow fruit of righteousness in you as you learn to tune into the voice of the Holy Spirit and yield to his direction as you move through your day.

Be aware of his presence in you.

He is gentle and does not yell, so it is up to you to listen for his promptings.

He will lead you into my truth.

He will lead you in the way I have planned for you.

He will instruct you in the way of holiness.

He will convict you of your bad choices and help you resist temptation by bringing to your remembrance my word, so you'll be able to ward off the enemy as he approaches—to strike him down with my word.

By this process, you will walk in step with my son, who has told you his yoke is easy; it is easy only as you walk in step with him.

Your response to the Holy Spirit makes this possible.

Be attentive to the still, small voice within you.

You will walk in love, joy, peace, and victory.

My beloved,

When temptations comes, you have opportunity to demonstrate who you believe and obey.

Do you yield to the demands of your natural person, the flesh and lies of Satan, or do you choose to deny the flesh and obey the Holy Spirit and my word?

When temptation comes, you must be quick to say (out loud if possible),

"I do not live for immediate gratification of my old nature"; or

"I choose to think and do what brings glory to God and what is good for me"; or

"I am a new creation, purchased by the blood of Christ, who paid my sin debt in full"; or

"I belong to God"; or

"All my needs are met by my God, Jehovah Jireh;" or

"My God supplies all my needs according to Christ's riches in glory."

Your lying tempter cannot resist the truth of my spoken word.

It cuts you free from Satan's tentacles that attempt to suck out of you your strength, joy, and peace.

Know my word of truth and use it often.

Keep practiced up at sword fighting.

Your victorious overcoming depends on you wearing the protective armor, holding firmly the shield of faith, and wielding the word-of-truth sword.

*Chapter 4*

# CORRECTION

My dear child,

You have just about given up.

You feel you've come to the end of life with nothing left to go on, nothing to go for.

But really, you have just begun.

Stop grumbling.

Stop complaining.

Cleanse your hands and your heart.

Trust me to lead you on right paths.

I will never, never, never leave you or abandon you.

Call on me continually.

Let me fill you with myself.

Let me fill your thoughts, your speech, and your actions.

Let me fully occupy your heart.

My beloved,

I live in you, and yes, I am mightier than all that would disturb you, all that is aimed at you to destroy you.

Fear not. I will be with you when you cry out to me in distress.

You will not just make it through, not just survive the ordeal, but you will come out of the ordeal with much knowledge, wisdom, and strength and a much deeper confidence in and reliance on me.

I am your father who loves you with all-encompassing love, an everlasting love.

There is nothing that can possibly come between you and my love for you.

My love is mightier than anything on earth or anything from the pit of hell.

You are mine, and you will be a jewel when I make up my crown in glory.

Fear not. You are in my hand, covered by my love.

My beloved,

I have promised, and I will keep my promises.

My truth is what sets you free as you mix it with your faith. With your heart, believe that it is true, not just generally but specifically for yourself.

Believe in your heart that it is true for your specific need.

I guide you into the truth, the specific truth that will help you apply the truth to your need and set you free.

My promises usually require your participation.

Do not quote my promises without participating in them.

My word is alive and active, so the recipient of my word must also be alive and active to enter into my truth for them.

Your faith—your counting on my truth to be a reality—is what unlocks the door to freedom.

Your knowing the truth is what sets you free. You're making it your own by faith is what sets you free.

My dear child,

I have a plan for each one.

No two plans are the same.

For each life, my plan is unique, so do not in any way compare the plan I have for you with plans I have for others.

The timing of events in each life is not haphazard but precisely timed by me and timed for a purpose.

Be still, stop fretting, and remember that I am God and I love you with a love much greater than you can possibly understand.

Nothing can separate you from my love.

To know me is life eternal.

Search my word, for in it I tell you of my love for you.

Some are dying for lack of love.

Receive my love and be a channel of my love to those in need.

My dear child,

Don't you know that I am God, and there is nothing—absolutely nothing—outside of my control?

I have called you to hate evil, but I've also called you to overcome evil with good.

It is a good thing to give praise unto your God.

Your discernment of evil is accurate, but your dwelling on it is robbing you of your joy.

Do not question my working in this; I'm at work, and I will accomplish my purposes in my time.

Know me and praise me.

Do battle by praising me.

My beloved,

Procrastination is disobedience.

I do not hurry you.

But remember, my timing is the best timing.

Your prompt obedience is what is best.

I will only give you one thing to do it a time—and time to do it.

I give you strength for today—and strength for your obedience one day at a time.

My beloved,

Those fruit-bearing branches who abide in Christ, I prune regularly so that they may bring forth more fruit.

Those things that I prune and remove from you are those things that sap your time, attention, and strength from your focus on me.

Your obedience to the call I have given you should be your top priority.

Do not encumber yourself with those things that do not minister to your being built up or do not give you opportunity to give others that which you have received from me.

I will lead you and guide you along the way, and I will also give you times of refreshment along the way.

I do not overburden you.

I have promised that as you are yoked and in unison with Jesus, at one with him, your burden or task will be light.

So, walk on with me, rejoicing, and with freedom and confidence in my faithfulness to my word.

My beloved,

There is a famine in the land, for the word of God is not being heard.

You are a well in the desert.

But the well is almost dry, and it's polluted with debris and waste materials.

There are cracks in the wall that must be mended and healed so that pollutants will not enter.

There is debris that must be washed away.

Let me cleanse and heal you.

Then I will fill you with living water so that you will become a fountain of life—my life.

Then those of the desert will come to you and drink of me and be cleansed and healed and strengthened.

Then the desert will bloom and bring forth fruit of righteousness.

My beloved,

Beware of busyness, even if it is for the kingdom of God.

Do not let the enemy ensnare you in the trap of legitimate consumers of your time and attention, to the detriment of your personal time with me.

Your time alone with me is very precious; guard it carefully.

I'm always with you, alone or in a crowd, but I desire time alone with you—just the two of us.

You can pour out your heart to me, and I receive it without question or condemnation.

I can speak to you those things that are the very best for you at the moment.

We get to know each other, and you get to know yourself by sharing yourself with me.

I love you, and I want our relationship to grow increasingly closer.

Come to me. You will never be disappointed, and your joy will overflow, and my joy and my love will splash onto others.

My beloved,

It takes practice to learn discernment.

You learn right from wrong and good from evil by the consequences of your choices in everyday living.

You are wired to be as I am.

Whenever you make the choice to please your old selfish nature and choose to do what is not in line with my character, my word, and my spirit, an alarm goes off in your spirit.

You must practice hearing and acknowledging that caution signal.

Train yourself to recognize it, identify it, and respond to it.

You can, by your will, override the caution signal and choose to sin.

You then operate on your own and at your own risk.

Your quick recognition and your owning of your sin, agreeing with me about it, and asking forgiveness removes it immediately and completely. It is gone, and I have forgotten it.

The plan is so simple. Even a small child can effectively practice knowing right from wrong and know how to come to me, ask forgiveness, receive forgiveness, and continue living as if this sin had not been commanded.

My little children learn by practicing to know right from wrong and continuing to practice doing right.

As you do, I'll watch and rejoice with you as you grow in grace and in the knowledge of Jesus.

*Chapter 5*

# FORGIVENESS

My beloved,

Be strengthened with forgiveness.

As I have forgiven you, so you must forgive one another.

I heal you through forgiveness.

You heal one another by forgiving one another.

You wound with your tongue.

Now heal one another with your forgiveness.

Do not withhold your forgiveness.

As much as you withhold forgiveness, this will leave part of my army weakened and open to attack.

I want a strong, vigorous army.

A soldier must be in top shape to withstand the rigors of battle.

So you must be strong for the battle that you are in.

I have given you the victory.

You must declare that victory in the land that I have given you.

The enemy will resist his surrender and will take full advantage of any wounds or weaknesses he sees in the individual soldiers of the occupying army.

Heal the wounds that you have inflicted on one another.

In your giving and receiving forgiveness, do not judge.

I alone judge.

As I have forgiven you, you must forgive one another.

My chosen ones,

Yes, I will cast all your sins into the deepest depths of the sea.

With great compassion, I will gather you to myself.

With everlasting loving-kindness, I will have compassion on you, says the Lord, your Redeemer.

I will forgive your iniquity, and your sin I will remember no more.

I have cleansed you, and I have anointed you with oil.

Your maker is your husband.

The Lord of hosts is his name.

The Lord delights in you.

As the bridegroom rejoices over the bride, so shall your God rejoice over you.

I have cleansed you, and I have anointed you with oil.

I have also clothed you with embroidered clothes, with royal robes and garments of fine, embroidered linen.

I have anointed you to bring good news to the afflicted.

I have sent you to bind up the brokenhearted, to proclaim victory to captives and freedom to prisoners.

I have brought you to myself.

I've caused you to grow like a vast number of plants of the field.

I have made a covenant with you: if you will obey my voice and keep my covenant, then you shall be my own possession among all peoples, and you shall be a special treasure to me.

My beloved,

I will betroth you to me forever.

Yes, I will betroth you to me in righteousness, loving-kindness, and compassion.

I will betroth you to me in faithfulness.

You will know the Lord.

I have cleansed you.

I have cast all your sins behind my back.

I pardon iniquity.

I delight in mercy.

I delight in unchanging love.

I have compassion for you.

I will tread your iniquities under my feet.

You will increase my joy and my delight.

You shall walk in a way of victory through turmoil, on a path that my hand has prepared for you.

You shall take the glad tidings of my deliverance to people held captive and in darkness.

Remember my promise, that the good work I began in you I will continue to bring to completion.

The gifts and calling of God are sure; they are not given and then taken back.

My giving is only limited or restricted by your willingness to obey me, your willingness to walk humbly with me, and your willingness to receive all that I have for you.

My beloved,

I love you with an everlasting love.

I love you with an unchanging love.

I love you with a love that cannot be destroyed.

I love you with a love deeper than the ocean and wider than the sky.

I love you with a love that is stronger than death.

I love you with a love that is gentle and warm.

I love you with a love that is quiet and calm.

I love you with a love that forgives.

I love you with a love that is powerful and pure.

I love you with a love that seeks the very best for you.

My love is unhindered.

As you freely accept my love, you will also learn to let my love flow through you to others, unhindered by fear, because you will learn that I alone am the one to meet all your needs, I alone am your security, and I alone am your love and life.

Come to me and know my love for you.

My love for you will heal your hurts.

My love for you will fill the emptiness in your heart.

My dear children,

Listen, listen, listen.

If my people listen, they will be led by me.

If my people listen with their hearts and desire to follow and obey me, they will hear my voice, and they will truly rejoice.

I will lead you, but only those who desire with their whole heart to yield to me will hear my voice.

Your dullness of hearing is an indication of your hardness of heart.

An obedient, yielded heart hears my voice and yields to my ways.

Turn back to me, and I will forgive and cleanse, and I will give you a new heart, a heart of flesh.

I will put my spirit within you and cause you to walk in my ways, and you will hear and heed my words.

My dear child,

If you love me, keep my commandments.

If you keep my commandments, you will abide in my love.

Do not tell me you love me and live as if you do not know me.

Many do not know me because you are too busy to spend time alone with me.

This is how you get to know me.

Spend time with me alone.

As you listen to me speak quietly to your heart, you'll get to know me and my love for you.

As you rejoice in thanksgiving for all I give you, we will celebrate together.

As you come to me for cleansing and refreshment, your love for me will deepen.

As you come to me for forgiveness, you will know my love for you.

As you come to me for comfort and encouragement, you will know my gentleness and my compassion.

As you come to me in your weakness, you will know my strength.

As you come to me in your failures and faults and receive my arm's strong support to sustain you, you will know that I love you.

Come to me at all times, in all conditions, and learn how I love you.

Come to me and learn of my love for you.

My love is gentle and patient.

My love is strong and everlasting.

My love can be rejected, but it cannot be destroyed.

My love can be taken for granted and neglected, but it can never be diminished.

My love was poured out on the cross and is available to you in its fullness each time you turn to me, especially when you return to me.

My beloved,

My child, why are you afraid of me?

Do you not know that Jesus took onto himself every one of your sins?

Because he did that, he took the full penalty of those sins when he suffered, bled, and died.

The price of your sins has been paid in full.

There is no condemnation for those who are in Christ.

Because of Jesus's blood and righteousness, you are free from the law of sin and death.

You are my child, and I love you.

You are very special, and I love you.

I've given you gifts that very few of my children possess.

Stop pushing me away.

I want to heal your wounds, for they are many.

I want to strengthen your inner self and equip you to tell others of my love.

I want you to tell others what Jesus has done for them because he loves them.

Some will not know of our love unless you tell them.

I have chosen you.

Stop running. Come to me. I love you.

*Chapter 6*

# RESTORATION

My dear child,

The long, dark night—will it ever end?

Yes, my child, the night will, as will the tears.

Soon now, you will see the first hints of dawn, and then you will see streaks of light coming through the clouds.

Do not despair, for I am still in control.

My way will be known, and my will shall be done.

You will rejoice in your God.

I will sustain you.

When your strength runs out, I will be your strength, so do not fear.

You are dear to me, and I will hold you up, and I will draw you to my heart, and you will rejoice at our closeness.

Rest now, and do not fret, for this thing is from me.

Trust me as I work silently in you and in others.

Be still and do not fear, for you are safe in my hand, and I will not let go of you.

Rest, my child, and know that I am faithful and true.

All of my grace and all of my love are yours.

Come into the ocean of my love.

Venture into the depths of my love so you will be enveloped and supported completely by my love.

Trust yourself completely to my love, for I am love.

I am yours, and you are mine.

My beloved,

Come to me without your mask that tells the world all is well.

Come to me without that shallow smile and determined look.

Come to me and level with yourself and me as to where you've been and what you've done, where you've gone off the track and gotten stuck, muddied up, bruised, broken, and trapped.

Come to me for cleansing, healing, restoration, and rest.

Come to me and learn again of my love for you.

Come to me, and my light will brighten your path.

Come to me, and my holiness will purify and strengthen your heart.

Come to me and rest secure in my sovereignty over your life.

Come to me and learn more and more of my great love for you, and learn to rest in my love.

Learn to delight yourself in your God, for your God delights in his own.

My beloved,

My precious child, my love for you is incomprehensible.

My love will heal your broken heart.

Let my love cleanse you of seeds of bitterness.

My plans for you are rooted in my great love for you.

Trust me as I work out my plans for you.

Draw close to me and learn of my love for you.

My dear child,

You have suffered, and you will suffer again, but do not lose heart.

Have I not been faithful to my promises to you all these years? Yes—and even before you looked to me in total dependence.

I loved you and watched over you, and I have been present with you through all of your life. From before you were born, I was with you.

You have not lived your life in vain.

You have suffered, and I will use that suffering to heal and redeem broken lives.

I am restoring and redeeming the moments of your life so that through your restoration others might have hope and faith to receive from me what you have already received from my storehouse of love.

Do not draw back.

Rest in the knowledge that I do nothing in you without a purpose.

That purpose is to restore, to heal, to free, to enliven with my love and with my life.

Rest quietly in my arms, close to my heart.

Don't be afraid. I love you, and I will never hurt you.

I will not permit you to be abused again.

You may get hurt by people but never the abuse of the past.

People may hurt you and cause you great disappointment, but you will not be abused as before.

As I have told you before, I will use you, but I have not said that you'd be popular.

Do not look to others for your worth, your satisfaction, or their approval.

Look to me. I will be your sufficiency in all of your needs.

Patiently obey my directions and do not be anxious.

My timing is perfect.

My beloved,

I cleanse and revive and heal and restore each one who agrees with me in their sin and turns from it, hurt and bruised with sorrow for their sin.

My love pours out on that one in concentrated form.

It is my love that brings wholeness to the broken ones.

Even so, my love flowing through you will bring life to those around you who are dying for the lack of love.

See how crucial it is for you to know and receive my love.

My love is not soft or mushy; it is strong and powerful in bringing change to those who receive it.

My love brings life, strength, truth, and victory over lies and deception.

Know my word. Know my love. Know me.

My beloved,

Jesus's obedience cost him his broken, bleeding body and separation from me.

Your obedience costs you the discomfort of denying the demands of your fleshly nature.

For some, obedience to my will costs them the death of their body, but as believers in Christ, they will never be separated from me.

Rather than separation from me, death will usher them into my very presence.

Pray for the martyrs of these days over much of the earth.

Pray for their steadfast reliance on me to the end, and pray for those they love and leave behind.

They do not die in vain, for some who persecute and kill my chosen ones will come to the truth of my redemption and repent and come to me.

Remember Saul, who met Jesus and became Paul.

That which is impossible with humans is possible with me.

Pray.

My dear children,

My kingdom is rising up all over the earth.

I'm calling my people to be kings and priests.

My people will intercede between me and those who are to be born into my family.

My kingdom increases each time one person is born into my family.

I will take the most unlikely, as far as humans are concerned, and raise them up to be mighty warriors.

Do not assign a particular potential to those or to yourself.

My plan for each person is so much greater than any person can imagine.

Simply come to me in your weakness and your limitations, yielding completely to my working in you.

Be ready to receive what I have in store for you.

You will marvel at my work and my plans.

There is no limit to what I can do with the totally surrendered life.

I have promised to complete the good work I have begun in you.

That work progresses as you choose to obey me in the smallest and greatest ways.

Do not be weary in doing what is right; your integrity is the basis on which I build your life.

My beloved,

Yes, my dear, I am the faithful keeper of my word.

Rest assured that all my promises to you are guaranteed.

That guarantee is written in the precious blood of my son, your Redeemer.

Every word of mine will be fulfilled—with no omissions and no oversights.

Continue to feed on my word and my faithfulness.

I will lead you, and I will keep you in the shelter of my wings.

Remember the little bird that was once struck down, dying; I scooped her up in my own hand and have nursed her back to increasing wholeness and strength.

You are that special one I've prepared to minister my love and my life to others who have been battered by the hurts of life.

You are a living example of my restoring power and of my tender desire to make the wounded whole.

Share my goodness to you with others, giving hope to those who at times feel that there is no hope.

Show them that hope in me does not disappoint.

My dear child,

I heal broken bones.

Can I not set a heart aright?

I heal broken hearts.

Let me heal your heart.

Let me heal you.

My love will fill in the broken places, restore the damage, and make strong your heart.

Be still and know that I am God.

I am the Lord that heals you.

My dear child,

Your days of mourning are ended.

I see your heart.

You shall have your heart's desire.

Go forward as Abraham, not knowing the land to which I lead you.

Lift up your head.

I bring you out of the pit of despair.

I will use you in mighty ways you cannot imagine.

Trust me. My plan is perfect, and my timing of that plan is perfect also.

Do not be anxious; you are in my hand.

Enjoy my gifts to you. The rosebud unfolds in beauty, not according to an imposed schedule but as it is designed and just when it's ready to blossom forth.

My dear child,

Do not despair.

That which is broken and bent, I will mend and straighten.

I will remove that which is not of me, and I will use the broken pieces of your life to build and restore to strength and beauty that which was once broken and scarred.

Light and love and healing will pierce the darkness of despair, and you will know the reality of my redemption of your life.

Strengthen your feeble knees by walking on.

I am with you to hold you and guide you.

Do not fear. I will not let you go.

I love you and will never abandon you.

You are mine, and I am yours forever.

My dear child,

I have given you my word.

Believe it to be true in the presence of all who say it is not true.

Real prayer sees the answer coming before it actually arrives.

The Lord said it.

The Lord will bring it about.

The Lord will be honored by it.

Faith in God can move a mountain.

Faith in God can calm life's troubled sea.

Faith can make a desert into a fountain.

Faith will bring life's victory.

Faith in God can change a dry, polluted well into a fountain of living water in the midst of a desert land.

My dear child,

When I lead you forth, I will make a way for you to walk.

The way may be steep and difficult, but I will be with you every step of the way.

The way may be long, much longer than you imagined, but do not give in to discouragement or despair.

I have promised you a land, a dwelling place, and I will bring you to that place that I have planned for you.

On your way to your promised land, you will be completed and prepared for my plans for you, and you will be healed of all that hinders your full freedom.

Trust me, for I am faithful to my word.

My dear, precious child,

I have brought you out of the horrible pit.

You will no longer walk with your head bowed down.

I lift your head up.

I will use you in a new and powerful way, a way you cannot imagine!

# EPILOGUE

The letters in this collection are expressions of the father's love for each of his children. God made each of us in his own image so that we might enjoy a loving relationship with him. The ultimate expression of his love was when he sent Jesus to do for us what we could not do for ourselves—that is, bridge the gap between the most holy God and sinful humankind.

Being human, we are born with a selfish nature, prone to sin. The Bible tells us that all have sinned and come short of his perfect standards, and that the end result of sin is death, which is separation from God.

Jesus came to pay the full penalty for our sin and for all sin. He died on the cross at Calvary in our place, so that we might be forgiven and spend eternity with him. When this happened, a great exchange took place.

Jesus received the evil we deserved, and we received all the good that he deserved. Jesus was punished that we might be forgiven (Isaiah 53:4–5). He was wounded that we might be healed (Matthew 8:17). He was made to be sin with our sinfulness that we might be made righteous with his righteousness (2 Corinthians 5:21). He tasted death for us that we might share his life (Hebrews 2:9). He was made a curse that we might receive blessings (Galatians 3:13–14). He endured our poverty that we might share his abundance (2 Corinthians 8:9). He endured our shame that we might share his glory (Matthew 27:35 and Hebrews 2:10). He endured our rejection that we might have his acceptance (Ephesians 1:3–6).

This is God's plan for each person, but each person must believe and receive this plan for themselves.

Here is how you receive God's forgiveness and new life in his family forever:

- Acknowledge that you are a sinner and that you need forgiveness.
- Believe in your heart that Jesus bore your sins on the cross, suffered, died, and was raised to life on the third day.
- Make a commitment to turn from your selfish ways and to follow Jesus, with God's help, all the days of your life.

When you do this, all heaven rejoices!

I welcome you to God's own family and pray that you will be saturated with his love and peace.

P.S. Start your new life by reading a modern translation of the Bible. Start reading the Gospel of John, or the Gospel of Mark. Next, find a Bible-teaching, people-loving church so that you may grow in your new life and enjoy sharing life with the Lord and his people.

May the Lord richly bless you.